Dedicated to the author's resolve.

M.D. Tophus

The A to Z of Workplace Bullying: For the Healthcare Professional and Beyond.

2

Hilphma Publications 2022. www.hilphmapublication.com

First Edition.

Germany.

The author has over 25 years of clinical experience in the healthcare field. Is cognisant of both DSM-5-TR (and previous versions) and ICD-11 (and previous versions) disorders and conditions; quality and safety improvement in healthcare; and healthcare education.

Sometimes workplaces are synonymous with the core elements of the Stanford prison experiment (1).
Bullying is an overused word, in modern day language, and thus is often reduced in intensity of meaning.

For many, it is substantial, real, and with everlasting deleterious affects.
To negotiate bullying behaviors is a task in itself. For those without the experience of such, they do not truly know the impacts.

Workplace bullying, especially in the healthcare sector, is not just consequential for the healthcare worker, but for the their team, their facility, and for their patients.

This publication covers the A to Z, literally, of the primary bullying modes and styles. It is aimed at informing for correct identification, classification, and comprehension, of bullying in (the workplace) all its forms.

It can also be used as a supportive resource for those currently, or historically, who experience such stressors.

In addition to covering collegial bullying, it examines multiple aspects of the dangers encountered by treating patients who assault, harrass, and, intimidate.

Other M.D. Tophus publications available:

"Exercising Quality in Healthcare Service Provision: A Complex Care Workbook for All Healthcare Professionals." Hilphma Publications: 2022.

"Who is This Colleague?: Dangers of the Healthcare Profession, and beyond. An Interview Guide for Recruitment, Performance Appraisal and Post-Adverse Events." Hilphma Publications: 2022.

"Think on your Feet: Those Who Can. For the Consummate Healthcare Professional." Hilphma Publications: 2022.

"The Unfortunate Healthcare Treater, The Hapless Healthcare Therapist: Narcissistic and Borderline Personality Disorder clients. The Grit." Hilphma Publications: 2022.

"Victims of Crime: Introduction to Forensic Challenges in Healthcare." Hilphma Publications: 2022.

CONTENTS

31   M: Malefic; malevolence; maliciousness; menacing; misogyny

33   N: Nark; nefariousness; nyaff

34   O: Obscene; obstructive; oppressing

35   P: Persecution; perverted; premeditated; pressurising; punitive

37   Q: Quarrelsome; querulousness

38   R: Remorselessness; repression; ruthlessness

39   S: Sabotaging; scaring; slander; snookering; splitting; stalking

41   T: Taunting; terrorising; tormenting; trash-talking

42   U: Unapproachable; undercutting; undermining; unrelenting; unremitting

44   V: Victim blaming; victim shaming; viperous; virulence

46   W: Wrath; wretched; wolfish

47   X: Xenophobic

48   Y: Yokelish

49   Z: Zealotry (weaponised).

The World Medical Association (WMA) has stated that violence against healthcare staff, and others working in health is "an international emergency that undermines the very foundations of health systems and impacts critically on patient's health" (2).

Healthcare work in emergency and psychiatric areas are highly impacted by violence toward staff. Many other healthcare environments continue to climb in risk status.
The affects are experienced by numerous different healthcare workers, however, frontline "doctors and nurses worldwide" (3) are particularly acknowledged.

A: Aggression; alienating; annihilating; antagonising; assault

Aggression: from colleagues

Psychological and verbal aggression are the most common forms of aggression experienced between staff in the healthcare field.

Although often associated with paternalism, and authoritarianism- threatening, intimidation, and belittling- can all be factors, at different levels, within the internal healthcare hierarchy.

Modes of aggression amongst healthcare colleagues can include: impingement upon personal space (face to face confrontation, uncomfortably close, demanding confrontations); removal of equipment forcibly; through to fist gesticulations, dangerous manoeuvres during patient treatment or

operative procedures; and, outright 'I will get you' gestures and comments.

These all factor into the categorisation of aggression from colleagues, and have vast impacts upon the next interaction with that same colleague, forward.

Alienation: intra/inter disciplinarily:

Disclosure of AEs and disclosure of near misses through to serious medical events (never events, for instance) are often perceived as outright whistleblowing, against co-workers, all healthcare staff personnel, and the establishment.

The backlash can be derived from some pseudo-philosophical loyalty based perception that quickly pervades every area of the particular health work environment.

That is, those who have reported shall never be trusted again.

With this, comes intra- and inter- disciplinary isolation, maltreatment, and questioning of one's moves ever after.

Alienation can take all forms, in this regard. From: 'miscommunications' about workplace meetings through to retracted important information regarding serious medical events which are headed for malpractice/medical neglicence claims.

This can be insidious, along with the colleagues involved.

Annihilating:

This involves attempts to destroy a healthcare workers career, and indeed have them removed from their position or bullying them to the point that they resign.
All manifestations of bullying are utilised in this regard.

Antagonising (interdisciplinarily):

Antagonism between interdisciplinary healthcare workers is an enduring phenomenon.
Collaborative efforts are well under way (in many healthcare environments) to consolidating firm co-operatives, interprofessionally.
However, the idea of bullying, fuelled by antagonising of fellow workers exists, regardless.
It is not as simple as different priorities held: due to differences in specialisation, knowledge and commitment.
The problems are often so ingrained that antagonistic behaviors, interdisciplinarily, become accepted phenomena. Thus, bullying is not acknowledged as such, nor called out.
Bullying can include withholding of essential communication and information, leading to an increased risk of adverse events.
Lack of respect and trust can lead to outright verbal abuse, and in some cases such severe hostility, which leads to: physical abuse; bad-mouthing and, damaging an interdisciplinarian's reputation.
Territorialism, feelings of superiority, and assumptions of poor (or inferior) training, are also at play.
Endemic, ingrained, and generational, rivalry- are inclusive of this.
To feign toleration, and yet victimise, is not a healthy alternative to the ideal- co-operation and collaboration.

Assault (in the workplace- patients and co-workers):

The effects of assault are experienced in different ways by healthcare personnel: injuries; leaving employment; trauma (and post traumatic stress); a change in attitude to work (from intrinsic to extrinsic motivators); burnout; effects upon attitude to patient safety and risk mitigation; and, therefore, an increased risk of medical errors.

In the majority of cases, verbal and physical assaults are perpetrated by patients. It is notable though, that (although less frequent) the assaults are inflicted by "relatives of patients, staff members"(4) or supervisors and managers of healthcare facilities.

Workers' compensation, mental breakdown, and mistrust of every colleague can be resultant of physical and verbal assaults suffered at the hands of a co-worker.
Although, many assaults remain unreported.

B: Barbed insults; battery; bias; brutalising

Barbed insults:

Barbed insults can be used to wear a co-worker down.

It is usually continuous, and often happens regardless of whether a fellow co-worker intervenes by stating (for instance) 'that's not nice'.

Typically, they include: personal insults (style of hair; makeup); insults regarding performance in healthcare such as- efficiency, effectiveness, and quality of skills, degree of knowledge, style of clinical practice, patient to patient interactions, and team meeting contributions.

Battery:

Battery in all its forms, has one commonality, that the actual wrongdoing is causing physical harm. This is the difference from assault, where there is the intent, and part of the impact being the fear of the intent.

Thus, when one considers patients presenting to emergency on ice (for example), the risk is real. Usually, the healthcare worker is informed of the fact, or derives the information from their own professional knowledge base.

The wrongdoing, in such a vein, from colleagues, is more muddied- at best. How does one predict an aggressive manoeuvre to an assault thence to battery?

It is questionable that any information on the subject, instantly applied, guarantees the healthcare worker- the protection- of which they are so deserved.

It crosses all boundaries, and when a patient (or a colleague) perpetrates upon that said healthcare worker- everything becomes theoretical.

Battery amongst healthcare workers is most associated with D.V. (for instance, when healthcare personnel are married/in a relationship, and work at the same healthcare facility).

Bias:

Much research has been undertaken regarding the impact of implicit bias and the varying levels of best practice based patient care undertaken by healthcare treaters, depending upon patients' race, age, gender, abled/disabled.
However, bullying of fellow healthcare workers occurs along similar lines.

This can manifest via bullying of:

healthcare workers with different (to the mainstream) cultural backgrounds; older versus younger trained healthcare staff (and vice versa); staff who have been overseas' trained (for instance); staff in relation to the area of the country from which the the training originated (socio-political and reputational focusses); workers who were trained by disliked, controversial, or de-registered professionals (they are often considered their continued lackeys).

Brutalising:

Managers and supervisors who are prone to bullying behaviors can impact healthcare workers maximally.
This can involve: denying the worker their due breaks during shifts; assigning unreasonably high (or difficult) work duties; scheduling long double shifts; minimal hours between shifts (no rest); no remuneration for overtime worked; expectations of healthcare professionals' endurance ad nauseum; inferred ultimatums such as the promise of promotion thwarted unless the staff member is compliant; threats about risk to licence and career; and, risk to employment status.

C: Coercion; corruption; cowing; cruelty; cussing; cyberbullying

Coercion:

Coercion of colleagues can be: bullying workers into performing duties in a controversial, non-standard way, or threats of collegial sabotage.

This extends to supervisors who threaten an employee with suspension, demotion, below pay level work duties, exclusion from team activities, or loss of job, unless they accede to daily force against their will, against protocol, and against what is set out in their individual healthcare professional clinical guidelines.

Coercion in the healthcare field is fuelled by feelings of superiority, power, and lack of accountability. It is regularly covered up via use of reasoning that forcing employees, and visiting healthcare staff, is purely KPIs based.

Corruption:

Healthcare workers who employ short-cuts in diagnosing, treating, and clinical decision making, who may be secretly funded to prescribe certain treatments or medications, usually bully and threaten other staff if they attempt to disclose the behaviors.

During pandemics, in particular, corruption can increase, as the focus shifts from anti-corruption measures to the basics of sustaining an overrun healthcare system.

Transparency and accountability play second fiddle to the short-term needs created by such a situation.

Corruption has many styles and modes: in some health systems, bribery of healthcare staff in order to access medical treatment is the norm; DRGs and other clinical data misrepresentations; double-dipping of healthcare treater payments; marginalising already vulnerable populations (by choosing to treat others instead); medical research and lack of transparent objectives and methods; punitive measures if any staff attempt to whistleblow; purposeful lack of support/inaccessability to healthcare worker support (in order to maintain the corruption).

Corruption in healthcare systems, is thus- in itself, bullying of patients and healthcare staff, alike, and has serious relentless consequences.

Cowing:

Intimidation of co-workers, or other healthcare staff, so that they cower to demands is not dissimilar to coercion.

The defining difference is that the intimidation is used to frighten the healthcare worker in the form of psychological abuse.

So in addition to the direct threats made, the success of this type of bullying tactic is the fear which pervades all areas of workplace performance in anticipation of more realised intimidation.

Cruelty:

This is a two-fold issue.

In some healthcare facilities exists cruelty toward patients by bullying staff, and often concomitant cruelty toward fellow co-workers.

Examples of verbal cruelty, for patients and healthcare staff, respectively: comments about lack of valuability in society, or within the health system; psychological cruelty: incitement of fear about a procedure, or that they will be labelled 'incompetent'; emotional cruelty: name-calling and purposely causing the individual embarassment in front of others; and physical cruelty: causing unecessary pain during a procedure, and grabbing of a healthcare worker forcibly.

Cussing:

Many people swear to let off steam.

This differs greatly from profanity used to make people feel uncomfortable, to acquiesce to their demands, to win an argument in anger, or used as a form of labelling of the worker.

This is then being utilised as a mechanism of bullying.

It may be that a cussing healthcare work colleague undertakes this face to face, or about other healthcare professionals; and that it involves harassing or discriminatory language.

Cyberbullying:

Cyberbullying patterns involve: texts, emails, social media platforms, and in chat rooms.
Once it starts, it is repetitive and often unrelenting.
Targetting of a healthcare individual causes trauma, difficult working environments, sickness, and burnout.
It is the constancy of this form of bullying which takes its toll on the victim.
It may be used to initiate team splitting, as a result of an ill-preferred choice of a newly recruited healthcare staff member, or as a perverse group cohesion tactic.
Additionally, healthcare groups, specialising in specific fields, as enclaves on social media platforms, may utilise premeditative planning for many other forms of bullying.

There is also the issue of cyberbullying instigated by disgruntled patients, patients' family members, or members of the wider community. The target, is in this instance, many differing interdisciplinary healthcare professionals.

D: Debasing; defaming; demoralising; dictatorial; domineering

Debasing:

Criticism of work performance daily and personal insults, can not only lower self-esteem, it can make you feel worthless and lose sense of dignity in and out of the workplace environment. The result: reduced to a tool, a thing, or just an obstacle to be 'leap-frogged' for another's (colleague, or supervisor) success.

Defaming:

False statements about an employee which can either be written, oral, or naturally both, is defamation at its basis.
That is, libel, and slander, respectively.
The impact: damage to patient referrals; loss of revenue; and, loss of job.
To illustrate: colleague spreads false rumours about a healthcare worker; or, negative reviews on social media sites, and numerous other modes.

Demoralising:

Workplace hostility, and in-fighting; unreasonable policies; leadership-induced fatigue; and,

bullying by management, leads to feelings of helplessness and risk of emotional exhaustion.

Dictatorial:

A bullying style of leadership, by specific healthcare professionals, who are autocratic and are fuelled by perceived hierarchical power, sometimes view themselves as the ultimate lifesaver of the healthcare facility.

To exemplify: the leader is self-focussed; is about maximal control; makes all decisions alone, without team input; and, reduces you to feelings like 'crushed like a small bug' if you attempt to offer a clinical opinion. Blame is also daily event.

This type of bullying impacts the entire team.

However, outspoken team members will become primary targets.

Domineering:

Although colloquially passed off as 'mr or mrs bossy boots' direct leadership, it is a serious problem when one is at the other end of a domineering force.

Typically, the lower the level of power the person holds (along with a chip on their shoulder),

the more likely that they will be domineering (as opposed to dictatorial).

It is definitely not just contained to some working in management positions in healthcare.

Just like the origins of trauma, generally, one cannot predict the resultant degree of traumatisation in individuals.

So too, domineering is no less upsetting than dictatorial bullying.

E: Enslaving; exploiting; explosive; extorting

Enslaving:

Exemplifications of 'enslavement' include:
low pay; working overtime without payment; threats from staff or managers that if you leave you will never get another job (bad reference, use of healthcare contacts). This could also fall into extortion.

Exploiting:

Good care, and, altruistic attitude, is rewarded (or rather, not rewarded) with: workplace shifts without breaks; unfillable services; nil reimbursement; and, low pay grades.
This can result in a feeling of being devalued, de-humanised, and so under-appreciated, that permanent demoralization sets in.

Explosive:

Intermittent screaming or shouting; yelling of abuse; and instances of rage type personality and behaviors by patients, or staff, is explosiveness at its best.
The temper release is almost always without warning.
There are no known boundaries as to how far their aggression will extend.

Extorting:

The 'extortionist' involves themselves in ransomware data attacks; allegiances, targetting specific healthcare professionals; false claims against healthcare staff from fellow co-workers, personnel; and receiving gifts, donations or monies, in exchange for medical care.
This amounts to bullying of healthcare professionals, and patients, similarly.

F: Fabricating lies; fear mongering; forcing; foul-mouthed; frightening

Fabricating lies:

Inciting others to lie, on behalf of the original perpetrator.

It is creation of the lie- the content within; the frequency; the extent; and, the purpose, which is the focus here.

Fear mongering:

Examples of this, include: creating trepidation if a colleague discloses, or does not comply with the fear mongerer's demands, that they will be: sacked; lose their position; be overlooked for a promotion; or, lose his/her licence.

Forcing:

Though similar to coercion, forcing implies complete non-negotiability with the perpetrator. Humiliation; manipulation; and, gaslighting- and multiple other methods- are utilised to continue the misuse of real, or perceived, power over the victim.

Foul-mouthed:

The 'foul-mouthed' bully perpetrates verbal abuse under the guise of letting of steam- not just swearing constantly, but personally directed telling of unwanted and environmentally inappropriate dirty stories; off limericks; and, for instance, debasing patients (regarding anatomical/physiological features).

Frightening:

Examples of this type of bully's behaviors are: yelling; closing in on physical personal space; violent outbursts; sabotaging work equipment; and, going through the victim's personal belongings. The end result of constant frightening can create panic, anxiety, high levels of stress, trauma, loss of concentration (as one is always looking over their proverbial shoulder), and reduced productivity.

G: Gaslighting; goading; greed

Gaslighting:

The ultimate aim is to make the victim question their sanity via psychological manipulation.
It can involve the perpetrator denying that things took place (conversations, actions, and decisions); sabotage, or lying, so that one incurs the punishment for the gaslighter's errors; belittling of you in public; constant- daily- negative feedback about work performance; and creating a target of rumours and innuendo.

Goading:

Incitement of the bullied to speak out, and then the inciter backs down (or does not back the healthcare worker) so that the victim stands alone, is the inherent nature of a 'goader'.
This is co-bullying, or aiding and abetting.
It can pertain also to when one discloses (or reports) adverse events (AEs); trouble within teams; as well as reporting a recalcitrant healthcare colleague.

Greed:

As known as insidious opportunism, the person will stop at nothing to achieve what they want to gain.
Bullying others frequently, in order to ensure strength and power, above colleagues is their modus operandi.

H: Harassing; hatefulness; hindering; hisogyny; hounding

Harassing:

Visual; written; and, verbal, the perpetration of harassing is insidious, relentless, and ultimately, (one hopes is acknowledged) of litigious proportions.

Hatefulness:

Extreme dislike expressed by animosity, is the hateful character.

Toxic comments and actions including via written expressions of hate in e-mails, staff meetings, perpertrated in front of patients, are often passed off as a personality clash/es.
It is, at the heart of many types of bullying.

Hindering:

Attempts to stop a healthcare colleague, or other, succeeding in the workplace is primary in this regard.
For instance: removal of PPEs through to double-booking treatments so that you are forced to internally triage, re-prioritise or de-prioritise risking patient safety, your work ethic, and leadership directives.

Hisogyny:

Particular targets, in the healthcare field, are: male nurses; and, male gynaecologists- though it definitely extends to other healthcare workers as well.
Assumptions about sexual preferences and identity; and, exclusionary actions by fellow staff, and patients- due to being male in a female dominated profession- are exemplifications of hisogynistic attitudes, and concomitant verbal abuse.

Hounding:

Even relentless 'nagging' takes its toll.
Especially, if it is a co-worker- and the victim themselves observes clear work boundaries.
For the hounder does not, they regularly cross them until you give in to their demands, listen to their endless troubles, and solve all of their problems.

I: Impunity; inciting; inexorable; insulting; intimidating

Impunity:

Due to leadership avoiding punishing or attempting to stop the bullying, there is further incitement to harassment, intimidation and negative behaviors.

Inciting:

Encouraging bullying, aiding and abetting it, and urging the bully toward violence and hatred, makes for a very difficult worklife for the victim.
Often, out of fear, protection of their own safety, or apathy, co-workers may stand by and allow this to develop (instead of taking pro-active steps to minimise the regularity of incitement before it comes to a head).

Inexorable:

Continuously oppositional is at issue here.
The inexorable person is very difficult to impossible to reason with; and, they present as incapable of being stopped in their pursuit of victimisation.

Insulting:

Often accompanied by confrontation, the regularly cited instances are of in-fighting between doctors and nurses.
Disrespectful comments and barbs, returned in kind, still constitute the classification of bullying.

It may appear mutual, but naturally one of the healthcare workers was the original perpetrator of the targetted insults.

Intimidating:

To create a feeling of foreboding, fearfulness, and terror, in a healthcare (or other), worker paralyses, shocks, and overwhelms.
When it moves to the physical, compliance is usually the reaction.
However, inaction and surrender, usually exacerbates the bully further.

J: Justice unrealised; juxtaposing

Justice unrealised:

Even when a report of harassment, intimidation, or a workplace violent incident is reported, and the report is formally documented and accepted, there are usually no repercussions for the bully. This is unless, perhaps, the bullying is continuous; the documentation is supported by collegial reports; and, the victimisation develops to the point of ongoing violent incidents.

Juxtaposing:

The juxtaposer makes constant comparison with the victim's others (colleagues, and so on) and presents the bullied in a negative light.
They pit one person against another, whilst the bully sits back and joyfully watches all their degenerative efforts play out.

K: Knavish; knocking down

Knavish:

Although used colloquially, as 'playful', the 'knave's' traits in the workplace environment are usually much more than this.

It most definitely is not a case of playfulness within healthcare.

Completely unprincipled, the knave lies repeatedly as a ruse.

They are untrustworthy to the point that they lure you again and again, and then fail you everytime (from team meetings to clinical applications of practice).

Knocking down:

Examples of this, include: repetitive criticism of the bullied's work performance, personal attributes, habits, gestures, and communication style.

L: Lewdness; libel (written defamation); lying

Lewdness:

Vulgar, sexualised behaviors and verbalisations; obscenities which can be non-sexualised but disturbingly gross, all the same, are at the core of the 'lewd' bully.
Exemplifications: singing 'off' things; obscene sayings; and/or otherwise known as a 'lech'.

Libel:

Written defamation of character in the workplace can extend as far as creating issues in gaining alternative employment.
False accusations are made either patient, or co-worker, and once it is circulated- there is an inherent problem, to say the least.
The false accusations can promote other forms of vilification toward the libelled.
Legal representation is a given.

Lying:

The aftermath of the fabrication of the mistruth.
Confabulated stories: to avoid accountability; to dodge clinical duties; to create mayhem within team environments; or, to impress (eg during work performance appraisals), are just some of the ways of this mendacious browbeater.

M: Malefic; malevolence; maliciousness; menacing; misogyny

Malefic/Maleficence:

The malefic bully threatens harm and causes intentional harm.

They are regularly termed 'evil'.

He/she is a risk to patient safety; purposefully and constantly endanger patients and colleagues as a core part of their clinical reasoning, judgement, practice, and personal beliefs.

The colleague is known as one to avoid- at all costs.

This is naturally not doable if you are required to work directly with them, in the same environment, clinic, or team.

Most, including supervisors, fear the malefic individual.

Thus, typically, they escape reprimand and suspension for their wrongdoings.

Malevolence:

Vengeful and hostile, with resultant harm desired, is quintessential malevolence.

It may be an inherent characteristic of the person. However, the acts of hostility are usually triggered by an event, a perceived sleight, or a belief of wrongdoing/misdirected concepts of injustice.

It creates a constant state of trepidation in their victim.

Malice/Maliciousness:

Malice on the other hand, is the intent of causing the harm.

That is, the cognitions and philosophy behind an action of harm; the lead up to the perpetration; and, the spite inspired aftermath.

Menacing:

Fuelled by, or indicated by, incidents of anger (either passive, or aggressive forms), threatening, is at the heart of the menacing. The perpetrator is typically considered a danger to be around, and is avoided (with differing degrees of success) by non-targetted colleagues.

Misogyny:

This can range from an inability to like women through to sheer hatred and intolerance of them. It is also represented by the belief that females are inferior to males, as absolute fact.
Sexism (in this case) can be categorised into: gender stereotyping, hostile sexism, and benevolent sexism (5).
One does not need to be a raging feminist to appreciate the implications of the 'misogynistic' bully. Misogyny affects female healthcare professional staff, and personnel, frequently; and, so too, the impact of this attitudinal trait (and actions) upon female patients.

N: Nark; nefariousness; nyaff

Nark:

Disclosure and whistleblowing differs vastly from an 'informant's' behaviors.

Whether real, or imagined, a 'plant' within the healthcare system who is assessing your every move, and comment, and reporting back to superiors, is a formalised bully- at best.

Examples of a nark: 'dobbing' like a schoolyard bully; creating mountains out of molehills; and, attributing blame disproportionately, whilst ignoring reporting true adverse events

Nefariousness:

Morally devoid of goodness is the nefarious individual.

The essential tenets of healthcare are: to do good; to do no harm; and, maintain this at all times.

A nefarious person is incapable of this as they are morally corrupted.

They are a risk to collegial safety, and patient quality and safety.

Nyaff:

Nyaff is originally a scottish term.

It is essentially a fightable person who are masking poor skills, and qualities, or have an inferiority complex.

They can make life most unpleasant for fellow co-workers.

They are usually unrelenting in their behaviors, and latch onto anyone that provides them with attention in relation to their fightability.

They cause no end of stress and disruption, especially in high care needs environments.

O: Obscene; obstructive; oppressing

Obscene:

The obscene bully is beyond lewd.

They intend to offend, and quite often with sexualised content, and always with out and out rudeness (beyond the often encountered coping based, and camaraderie driven, warped sense of humour of some healthcare professionals).

If you are the brunt of their jokes, comments and gesticulations and express disfavour and disgust, yet it nevertheless continues, then this is evidentialised bullying.

Obstructive:

An obstructive person creates difficulties intentionally.

This includes protracting clinical decision making, treatment, and response to co-worker communications.

They throw a proverbial spanner in the works, at every turn.

He/she is harrowing, and almost impossible to deal with.

Oppressing/Oppressive:

Some leadership staff, whether a team leader or in upper management, can be harsh and unfair.

However, in modern day, each co-worker is ideally encouraged to take a leadership role.

Thus, act of oppression can be played out by fellow co-workers.

They can create stress, exhaustion, and lead the victim toward burnout.

P: Persecution; perverted; premeditated; pressurising; punitive

Persecution:

When a healthcare worker dares to complain, or even externally discloses, about lack of PPEs or anti-risk mitigation working conditions (for instance), they can become a direct target at the hands of their own healthcare system.
In some regions this has direct human rights implications (in addition to workplace law).

Perverted:

The perverted bully perpetrates out and out sexual harassment; is sexually suggestive; makes sexualised comments directly to (and about) the victim; propositions the bullied in a sexual way; and makes sexual advances, physically.
Lawyer time (as with many other forms of relentless bullying), if management, human resources/ occupational department, or your professional body, are unhelpful.

Premeditated:

Premeditative bullying, for authoritarian reasons, responses to personality clashes, or to climb the proverbial ladder, manifests in many different ways.
From the outset, it will invariably be daily; will vacillate from put-downs and belittling; and, extend as far as non-impulsive, pre-planned physical violence.

Pressurising:

Meeting unrealistic KPIs or, being required to quickly respond to and record accurate DRGs, are two examples of bullying style pressurisations.
When the healthcare facility: lacks the resources, and staff; has time pressures (which result in best clinical practice being re-prioritised with de-prioritisation of essential work duties); has unsuitable staff-patient ratios; or, pressurises the healthcare worker to the maximum, this creates a highly
stressful environment and impacts each healthcare worker, personally.

Punitive:

A disconnected approach by leadership which results in the threat or realisation of constant punishment, even for the smallest of administrative mistakes, can certainly take its toll.
It can lead to high levels of absenteeism and low work retention rates.

Q: Quarrelsome; querulousness

Quarrelsome:

A quarrelsome bully easily brings their trouble-making to the point of causing major team in-fighting.

Fighting due to competitiveness, jealousy, or for dramatic effect, are not just personality traits. The perpetrator is aware of the harm that they are doing, and continues anyway.

Querulousness:

Constant complaining about fellow healthcare workers, as in whingeing about healthcare colleagues' habits, personal likes and dislikes, and holding onto unproven (or inconsequential) grievances, can put pressure on the individual.

It is a selective form of bullying, which often has intent beyond the apparent smallness of their complaints.

It is the frequency and unpredictability of the apparent offense taken, by the complainer, which especially takes its toll on their victims.

R: Remorselessness; repression; ruthlessness

Remorselessness:

When the individual has no capacity for guilt regarding their negative actions, their medical errors, and their poor clinical decision making (which affect patients, and the colleague's team, alike), then there is minimal chance of reasoning with them about: accountability; learning from their mistakes; or, finding common ground with them.

Repression/repressive:

It can be disclosure about AEs, about bullying itself, or the danger of a colleagues' chosen clinical practices, with which repression emerges.
The suppression of reports; and/or expressed concerns to direct leaders, and beyond, creates feelings of stress, distrust, and trepidation about future support being unprovided.

Ruthlessness:

This has similarities with 'cruelty' but involves lack of compassion- at the forefront.
Brutality toward patients is often a warning indicator of what may later be experienced by colleagues.

They also have no fear of reprisal; and regularly target co-workers who they feel may recognise their incapacity for remorse.

S: Sabotaging; scaring; slander; snookering; splitting; stalking

Sabotaging:

Many other forms of this have have been covered in this publication.
Taking credit for another's work; excluding the victim from written and verbal team communications; and, inciting further intimidation by telling lies about colleagues hating you, are just some of the forms a 'saboteur' will employ.
This also includes, corporate sabotage: (that is, your previous boss attempts to impede your future work opportunities).

Scaring:

Often considered the ward clown- but with an (malicious) edge when you are the target of it- scaring (as in giving frights), scaring by creating stories/imagined risks which upset fellow staff (even if they eventually say they are joking), is still a form of bullying.
The perpetrator usually has a perverse need to scare, and cannot function without it.

Slander/slandering:

This is essentially, spoken defamation.
In illustration: harmful speech about job performance; application of clinical practice; and, communication style.
Personality; and mental acuity, is additionally integrative.
Capacity to continue working (affecting number of referrals; and practice as a whole), is ultimately at issue.

Snookering:

Tricking co-workers into difficult positions, and then leaving them to clean up the proverbial (or literal) mess, is at the core of snookering.
It could be that you are lured away from your planned work duties, to help with a difficult patient; and, then the bullying colleague leaves you alone to deal with them, through to- purposeful sabotage of clinical practice, which one ends up at 'an end' or is forced to leave unresolved.

Splitting: as in within, and between teams

Splitting team members is considered a life-long pursuit, by some in healthcare. It becomes like a game which they enjoy, a game which yields much damage inter and intra the team involved.
Undercutting or bad mouthing other team members, and spreading rumours are some of the vehicles used to break a cohesive team.
The aim can be revenge toward one of the team members, or purely to break all co-operation.

Stalking:

This can additionally involve defamation of character.
It is following (or, forward following); threatening to victimise family and friends, or property; and, lying to obtain personal details about the victim to further the stalking behaviors.
It is a known issue within workplaces; and the double-threat of patients with these traits, makes for unsettling contemplation.

T: Taunting; terrorising; tormenting; trash-talking

Taunting:

Relentless provocation; annoyance; and, teasing in the workplace, is never good.
When undertaken in front of other staff (for instance, whom one is training), this most certainly 'ups the ante'.

Terrorising:

This is the culmination of many fear-based bullying tactics.
It is intended to create ongoing anxiety, in order to weaken the individual into surrendering to their demands, and accepting the bully as dominant, forever.

Tormenting:

Many who have experienced trauma and/or burnout recall the continuity of anguish that they felt at the hands of their bullying perpetrator.

Trash-talking:

Trash-talking is a style of verbal assault which is planned to humiliate.
It can also take the form of a braggard, who insults the victim, by competing claims (usually lies) about the grandeur of their work performance in comparison with your own.

U: Unapproachable; undercutting; undermining; unrelenting; unremitting

Unapproachable:

From simple aloofness to menacing, the impossible healthcare colleague is this.

Take heed of the obvious in this circumstance.

Adoption of: third party avenues of communication, where possible, are necessary, or finding

a go-between who has found a way around this type of bully.

Undercutting:

There is worker to worker subjugation; and, there is management who undermine, thwart, and

erode trust ad infinitem.

Undermining:

The aim of undermining is to slowly erode any dignity, self-confidence, or sense of satisfaction

and purpose which the victim holds personally, or via their healthcare work commitments.

Unrelenting:

This is more a mode of browbeating.

Implacable and dogged, the 'unrelenting' lives to bully as opposed to bully to live.

Intrinsic motivation to the maximum.

Unremitting:

A persistent bully, saboteur, and complainer, who finds every way to avoid being foiled in their recalcitrant efforts is the 'unremitter' to a T.

V: Victim blaming; victim shaming; viperous; virulence

Victim blaming:

If the victimiser is highly productive and impactful (upon for instance, KPIs), then the manager
is most likely to overlook their subjugating tactics toward the victim/s.
This promotes prejudice toward the victimised individual/s.
It encourages similarly repeated behaviors, by the bullied's colleagues.
This can expand to wrongly labelling the impacted as bullies, themselves.
This leads to the next categorisation.

Victim shaming:

'Why did you let it continue so long?'
'Why didn't you ask for help?'
'If you are innocent, why didn't you just say so, it would have changed everything'
'What have you done to help yourself, since the victimisation?'
'Do you have skeletons in your closet which you don't want revealed?'

Viperous:

Jealous, malevolent and resentful, regardless of the reason for such, is the 'viperous' bully.
Usually envious to the 'nth- degree', they will toxify every facet of the workplace environment, to
the point of no return.
Facilitating their departure from the workplace is the only feasible option available.

Virulent/Virulence:

Embittered (by jealousy; or, a perceived wrong-doing which has impacted them) is the 'virulent'.
They harbour resentment to the end.
If it involves a sleighted patient, or caregiver, who has been wronged or, a healthcare staff
member placed in an unenviable position, the acrimony is/will be palpable.
Beware.

W: Wrath; wretched; wolfish

Wrath/Wrathful:

Extreme anger (with or without the aggression), and deep resentment, usually fuels vengeful actions of this kind of bully.

Wretched:

Not to be confused with genuine pain and anguish, people tend to over-compensate for this type of perpetrator because of their explained suffering.

The manipulation ranges from: not being able to perform tasks because of their ongoing (usually personal) upset through to literally and regularly walking off the job.

If this continues for some time, and one speaks with their colleagues and only certain (more empathetic persons) are their target, then the answer is almost definitely that this is a form of bullying. That is, via manipulation, negotiation, lying, and pulling on the 'heart-strings'.

Exemplification of the wretched bully: the affliction and misery deleteriously affects others; borderline personality type symptomatology; is needy beyond the usually expected workplace support; draws everyone in to their dilemmas (or selective sympathetic few); is unbending and constant; wears colleagues down; and, places healthcare workers at risk of absenteeism, exhaustion and burnout.

Wolfish:

Often charming, likeable at face value, there is an inhumanity about the 'wolfish' individual.

This poses a problem, especially when one is working in life or death environments such as within the healthcare field.

Voracious in their pursuits, usually regarding career aspirations, where the power level of their fellow workers matters not, they will stop at nothing to get what they want- usually, leaving many a damaged career of co-workers behind them.

X: Xenophobic

Xenophobic:

Amongst healthcare workers, although aligned with 'bias' the 'xenophobe' is more intensely attitudinalised than in simple cultural biases, and often extends beyond the typical parameters of cultural background biases.
Racial prejudice toward patients (or medical xenophobia) can involve: "alienation of minorities due to racial supremacism and lack of empathy" (6).
This can jeopardise effective healthcare treatment.

Migrants, the homeless, and other vulnerable groups, are at risk of being victims of poor or no healthcare treatment; and, being labelled negatively. This can be further exacerbated when a healthcare system is overrun.
This pertains not just to leadership but to frontline workers' attitudes who hold implicit or explicit biases towards certain races and cultures.

Examples of xenophobia extend from attitudes and behavior toward patients to fellow co-workers.
For instance, that non-white doctors are: "actually not physicians; inappropriate comments about.. race, and structural biases that led to substantially fewer advancement opportunities" (7).
Linguistic history, or language differences, also play a part in this.

Y: Yokelish

Yokelish:

Rudeness and ignorance personified, this type of person is an unwitting bully.

They are aware that they are doing it, but know no better (or believe so).

Capable of learning every other task, style, and form of communication, they are very stubborn

when it comes to repeated, requested changes to their manner, comments and behaviors,

regardless of whether the sufferers are impacted, and by how much.

Z: Zealotry (weaponised).

Zealotry:

In relation to healthcare service providers, and admission of (for example) non-religious patients into religiously funded healthcare facilities, the following requires explicating.

There are:

"Four perspectives on helper orientations- religious rejectionism, religious exclusivism, religious constructivism, and religious pluralism- can be adopted by health practitioners that reflect different positions as to the validity of the clients' religious orientation and its significance for treatment" (8).

However, religious exclusivism often prevails in religiously funded healthcare organizations. This can deleteriously affect patient admission, care and treatment, when a patient who is not religious asks for help.

So too, with this attitude, comes the negative effects on non-religious healthcare staff.

Behaviors of which unfortunately constitute two-fold bullying, to say the least.

The impact on healthcare colleagues: the 'zealot' bully weaponises religion as a tool: to intimidate; isolate other team members; to avoid accountabilty for actions (and believes they are protected because of healthcare system guidelines regarding faith-based choices); or, to undertake ill-advised conscientious objection.

They impact entire teams, and associated interdisciplinary teams; are immovable in their clinical reasoning; and, cause co-workers to compensate for choices made.

This causes ongoing stress, with the victims looking over their shoulder frequently to see the next anti-team, and often anti-risk mitigating choice, that they will make.

Another form of bullying, indeed.

PLEASE NOTE:

With all stated above, with the level of intensity purveyed, it must be noted that there are many avenues by which one can challenge bullying behaviors in workplaces, and with special focus on the healthcare environment.

In many regions, there are (in addition to occupational departments/human resources): hotlines; advice centers; written pamphlets, and other publications; professional network legal representatives; and, ofcourse, your trusted colleagues, which you can turn to for support; information; and, who can provide vehicles to assist in stopping the bullying behaviors from recurring.

ABBREVIATIONS; EXPLANATIONS

AEs: Adverse Events

DRGs: Diagnostic Related Groups

D.V: Domestic Violence

KPIs: Key Performance Indicators

REFERENCES

(4) Babiarczyk, B., Turbiaz, A., Tomagova, M., Zelenikova, R., Önler, E. and Sancho Cantus, D. Violence against nurses working in the health sector in five European countries- pilot study, Int.J.Nurs Pract. 2019 Aug. 25(4): e12744, www.pubmed.ncbi.nlm.nih.gov

(8) Chatters, L.M. Religion and health: Public health research and practice, Annu.Rev. Public Health, 2000; 21:335-67.

(5) Mesquita Filho, M., Marques, T.F., Rocha, A.B.C., Oliviera, S.R., Brito, M.B. and Pereira, C.C.Q. Sexism against women among primary healthcare workers, Cien Saude Colet. 2018, Nov; 23(11):3491-3504.

(7) Serafini, K., Coyer, C., Brown Speights, J., Donovan, D., Guh, J., Washington, J. and Ainsworth, C. Racism as experienced by physicians of color in the health care setting, Fam. Med., 2020; 52(4):282-287.

(6) Sim, W., Lim, W.H., Ng, C.H., Yaow, C.Y.L., Cheong, C.W.Z., Khoo, C.M., Samarasekera, D.D., Devi, M.K. and Chong, C.S. (2021), The perspectives of health professionals and patients on racism in healthcare: A qualitative systematic review, PLoS ONE, 16(8):e0255936, pdf, pp:1-15.

(3) Vento, S., Cainelli, F. and Vallone, A. Violence against healthcare workers: a worldwide phenomenon with serious consequences. Frontiers in public health, Sept. 2020, 8:570459, pdf:2.

(2) World Medical Association. 73rd world health assembly, agenda item 3: COVID-19 pandemic response, (2020), www.wma.net/wp-content/uploads/2020/05/WHA73-WMA-Statement-on-Covid-19-pandemic-response.pdf

(1) Zimbardo, P.G., Maslach, C. and Haney, C. (2000), Reflections on the Stanford prison experiment: Genesis, transformations, consequences. In Obedience to authority: Current perspectives on the Milgram paradigm, Chapt. 11. Blass (Ed.). USA: Lawrence Erlbaum Publications, pp.193-237.